A LEXICON
SOCIOLOGICAL
TERMS & THEORISTS

SECOND EDITION

JOHN S. KNOX

Kendall Hunt
publishing company

Kendall Hunt
publishing company

www.kendallhunt.com
Send all inquiries to:
4050 Westmark Drive
Dubuque, IA 52004-1840

Text alone ISBN: 978-1-5249-8950-7
PAK ISBN: 978-1-5249-8809-8

Published in the United States of America

For Sir Ben,
my doctoral studies
supervisor extraordinaire.

CONTENTS

ILLUSTRATIONS

PREFACE

Why compose a dictionary of important sociological terms and theories? Simply, my inspiration came from a statistics textbook that I was assigned to read for a required graduate class in Sociology. Let's just say that I was completely *underwhelmed* by the anemic and enigmatic definitions for key sociological terms that the textbook author provided in each chapter (and in the glossary). Moreover, when I went outside of the textbook to search other online dictionaries and other books for clear definitions, I was frustrated with their sparse offerings and explanations, too. I thought to myself, if this is challenging and frustrating for me—and I have a PhD in Theology and Religion, how difficult must this be for students just out of undergraduate studies?

Part of understanding Communism comes from understanding Karl Marx's life; part of understanding gender studies comes from understanding Harriet Martineau's culture; part of understanding race relations comes from understanding Booker T. Washington's journey, etc. Sociologists may be social scientists, but like everyone else on earth, they are human beings operating under the same sociological forces that they investigate and theorize about during their careers. And their life stories, like their theories, often provide insight to human interactions in society.

At that moment, I felt inspired to write a better, more comprehensible lexicon of terms and important people in the field of Sociology for my students. People cannot learn if they are not provided with understandable explanations or descriptions, which is the main goal of this book. Thus, whenever and wherever possible, I tried to use uncomplicated, straightforward terms in the definitions.

One more thing: this is the second edition of my *Lexicon of Sociological Terms and Theorists*. A chapter on the sociology of religion was added in, but additional chapters are planned and sure to come in the future. More words, charts, and chapters will be added (and hopefully other cool illustrations), where needed. Some definitions and descriptions may need sharpening and clarifying, but I expect and welcome this. Buying textbooks is expensive enough without spending money on books that fail to do the one thing that they are supposed do—Sharing. Knowledge. Comprehensibly. That has been, and will continue to be, my goal in the classroom and in my writings.

ACKNOWLEDGMENTS

First and foremost, I offer my heartfelt gratitude to my old schoolmate and friend, Daniel Schallau, for sharing his amazing artistic talents to help me visually reach and teach my readers about the ways and "whos" of Sociology. He is so good at illustration that it is hard to believe that we took the same drafting and art classes in high school some thirty-five years ago. Dan's artwork has helped bring my words to life. Thank you, sincerely.

Second, and yet again, I appreciate the editorial and proofing assistance of my former George Fox University student and friend, Heather Harney (this is book six for her); and my comrade, former racquetball partner, and local Nampa pastor, Keith Freedman (this is book five for him). To both of you, thank you for your savvy editorial suggestions, and for your willingness to read over yet another of my books. I come back to you, time and time again, pleading for more editorial appraisals, out of deep respect for you both.

Of course, once again, I could not have completed this book without the on-going support and love of my wife, Brenda, and my very patient sons, Jacob and Joe. Writing a book takes time, and I appreciate their letting me have that time to go into my "cave' to think and write and edit, and then to think and write and edit some more. I promise to buy you lots of toys and computer games, though, with all my royalties.

CHAPTER ONE: Introduction

Agency: This term refers to the freedom of choice and behavior that all human beings possess in life.

Anomie: Coined by Émile Durkheim (French, 1858–1917), this term denotes the sense of social powerlessness and disorientation when a person feels that his or her social influence and/or control is useless and ineffectual.

Applied Sociology: Rather than merely a systematic study of human interactions and behaviors, applied sociology seeks to provide practical advice, change, and solutions (outside of academia) for people in social need or in dire straits.

Clinical Sociology: Not just an academic or intellectual study of human interactions, clinical sociology seeks to change or improve specific aspects of troubled social relationships for institutions or groups.

Common Sense: This form of knowledge may be accurate (or not), based on a customary but not systematic analysis of facts.

Comte, Auguste: A popular (though mentally unstable) figure in nineteenth-century European culture, Comte (French, 1798–1857) officially coined the term, "Sociology" in 1838, and started the Church of Humanity in 1878.

Conflict Perspective: Tied closely with Karl Marx (German, 1818–1883), the author of the *Communist Manifesto*, conflict perspective suggests that all human interactions and social problems are enveloped in and driven by social conflict, competition, and contention for economic and political resources.

Dramaturgical Approach: A view of social interaction popularized by Erving Goffman (Canadian-American, 1922–1982) wherein people are considered to be like theatrical performers regarding their social roles and experiences.

Durkheim, Émile: Famous for his penning of the term, "Anomie," Durkheim (French, 1858–1917) was one of the most influential founders of Sociology and Anthropology—especially regarding religion, methodology, and suicide.

Epistemology: This is the theory or study of facts or information gained from a figure authority, personal experience, cultural tradition, the mass media, scientific forums, or personal faith.

Functionalist Perspective: Originating with Émile Durkheim (French, 1858–1917), the functionalist perspective takes an organic approach concerning how complex social structures maintain their stability, suggesting that every person, by playing their part in the social structure, contributes to its health or functionality.

Globalization: Centering mostly on economics (and with ties to Conflict Theory), globalization focuses on how all nations are influenced and affected (both negatively and positively) by foreign governmental policies, financial markets and goods, technological innovations, the exchange of cultural ideas, and indigenous social movements.

Human Behavior: Refers to the various activities of human beings biologically, intellectually, and socially, which are influenced by a variety of intrinsic and extrinsic factors such as emotion, IQ, genetics, age, gender, culture, etc.

Interactionist Perspective: Penned by Herbert Blumer (American, 1900–1987), the interactionist perspective (also known as symbolic interactionism) is a sociological approach suggesting that all people utilize symbols, social artifacts, and common cultural connections to communicate and coexist with others in everyday social relationships.

Macrosociology: A branch of Sociology that holistically focuses on sociological phenomena and whole cultures/civilizations.

Microsociology: A branch of Sociology that investigates small groups and their social environments, typically through scientific research and experimentation.

Natural Science: A branch of science that focuses on understanding and explaining natural phenomena through scientific methodology, experimentation, and observation.

Private Troubles: Personal obstacles that individuals face as individuals rather than as a consequence of their social position.

Public Issues: Community obstacles that individuals in similar positions or groups encounter; they are also referred to by sociologists as "social problems."

Science: The systematic study of the natural world that utilizes scientific methodology, experimentation, and observation.

Social Inequality: Historically occurs when members of any society possess varying amounts of wealth, social clout, and political power.

Social Psychology: The study of the individual human mind and how social groups influence and affect it (for better or worse).

Social Science: The systematic, scientific study of all human interactions and relationships.

Social Work: Involved more in the applied sciences realm (although resting philosophically upon accepted sociological theory), social work seeks to remedy systemic or deeply ingrained sociological problems in society.

Sociological Imagination: Coined by C. Wright Mills (American, 1916–1962), sociological imagination utilizes purposeful, creative, sometimes external reflection concerning the forces and causes involved in social interactions and attitudes for the individual and greater society.

Sociological Perspective: An awareness that sociological context affects and influences both individuals and groups in society

Socialization: An ongoing, lifelong process wherein all people learn and develop beliefs and behaviors deemed acceptable and/or necessary to exist in a specific culture or community.

Social Problems: When a condition (or conditions) is perceived to be harmful to society (such as crime, racism, poverty, pollution, etc.), and new strategies are employed to actively bring an end to the problem.

Sociology: A term coined by Auguste Comte (French, 1798–1857), the branch of science that focuses on the systematic study of all human social behavior, interactions, and relationships (collectively and individually).

Systematic Sociological Study: Relying upon empirical data and scientific methodology, the overarching, categorical process or program to investigate the social interactions between people.

Theory: In Sociology, a speculative belief or a set of suppositional principles that are used to explain the causes and consequences of social problems, human attitudes, or behavior.

Weber, Max: Considered by many to be the founding father of Sociology, Weber (German, 1864–1920) was a trained lawyer who used his keen intellect and embrace of scientific methodology to study capitalism, bureaucracies, and the social sciences.

Discussion Questions

1. What is Sociology? What does it include?
2. How is Sociology different than Common Sense?
3. What is the difference between Public and Private matters?
4. How did social, biological, economic, and psychological factors affect your choice to attend your university?
5. How can Sociology help a person understand the world, today?

WHEEL OF SOCIOLOGY

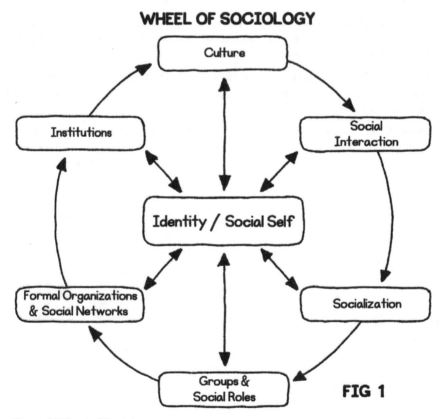

Figure 1: Wheel of Sociology

Source: John Knox and Daniel Schallau.

CHAPTER TWO: Sociological Research

Breaching Experiments: Often utilized in sociological research, the exposure to pre-selected behaviors, while the researcher purposefully withholds the basic assumptions of the situation or experiment in order to observe the responses/reactions of the subjects of study.

Causal Logic: The cause-and-effect relationship between social conditions/variables and specific consequences.

Case Studies: A research approach that relies upon close, personal observation of social behavior, beliefs, and culture.

Code of Ethics: A guideline of moral principles established and regulated by members in a profession (such as the American Sociological Association).

Content Analysis: The coherent, objective, methodological recording and review of coded data.

Control Group: The participants or subjects in a social experiment who are purposefully isolated and/or excluded from exposure to an independent variable.

Control Variable: A sustained communal or individual factor used to test the social significance of an independent variable.

Correlation: The connection between two or more variables in which changes for one variable coincides with a change in another (or others).

Data Collection: The gathering of data—through random, systematic, or stratified sampling—concerning a group of people being studied, sociologically.

Dependent Variable: The variable in a causal relationship that is subject to the influence of another variable.

Ethnography: A holistic scientific study of a cultural environment regarding individual responses and prioritizations in social interactions.

Ethnomethodology: A term coined by Harold Garfinkel (American, 1917–2011) for the study of rules that people follow in everyday social interactions.

Experiment: A scientific directed assessment that provides researchers with positive and negative results regarding sociological variables, discoveries, and hypotheses.

Experimental Group: The participants or subjects in a social experiment who are purposefully exposed to an independent variable to measure their responses (or lack thereof).

Hawthorne Effect: When participants in a scientific study alter their behavior because they are conscious of being observed by researchers.

Hypothesis: A testable statement about the relationship between two or more variables or factors.

Independent Variable: The variable in a causal relationship that causes or influences a change in a second variable.

Interview: Typically done face-to-face, a scientific interrogation of a participant in a sociological study to gather more qualitative than quantitative data.

Mean: A number calculated by adding a series of values and then dividing by the number of values. For example, for 4 + 4 + 2, the mean would be 3.333 (or 10 ÷ 3).

Median: The midpoint or number that divides a series of values into two groups of equal numbers of values. For example, for 5 + 5 + 3 + 2 + 1, the median would be 3.

Mode: The single most common value in a series of scores. For example, for 5 + 5 + 3 + 2, the mode would be 5.

Observation: Rather than interviewing or surveying participants to gather data, researchers collect information by closely monitoring the sample population without direct contact or engagement with them.

Operational Definition: A statement that clearly conveys the procedures used in testing a relevant sociological problem or theory regarding a specific variable or concept.

Population: The target group focused upon in a sociological research project.

Qualitative Research: Focuses more on the compilation and analysis of individualized data to provide insight on personal characteristics, attitudes, and activities in a specific sociological environment.

Quantitative Research: Focuses more on the compilation and analysis of numerical data to provide insight on larger demographic sociological environments.

Questionnaire: A printed or written question sheet used to acquire qualitative and/or quantitative data from respondents.

Random Sample: A sample of a population in which each participant is chosen in arbitrary fashion, providing an equal chance for all people within the sample to be selected.

Range: The difference between the highest and lowest values in a set of numbers. For example, for 5 + 3 + 2 + 1, the range would be 4 (or 5 − 1).

Reliability: How much a measure or scale consistently evaluates a sociological factor or force under examination.

Research Design: A comprehensive, carefully-fashioned procedure that utilizes scientific methodology for investigating a sociological problem or theory.

Sample: A small cross section of a specific group of people that is statistically representative of that overall population.

Scientific Method: The methodological procedure in scientific research studies that relies upon objective observation and active manipulation to accurately test a sociological theory or question.

Secondary Analysis: A method of research that relies more upon previously collected sociological data to investigate a sociological problem or theory than any new, additional, active, on-going research efforts.

Survey: An investigation utilizing interviews or a question set to gather sociological data regarding a specific sociological question or theory.

Validity: How much a measure or scale accurately explains a sociological factor or force under examination.

Value Neutrality: A term used by Max Weber (German, 1864–1920) that refers to the pursuit of objective interpretations of data in Sociology.

Variable: A measurable trait or element that is subject to change in different environments or conditions.

Discussion Questions

1. Why is sociological research necessary in academia?
2. How is the scientific method utilized in sociological research?
3. What are some of the dangers of sociological research?
4. How is survey data different than observational data?
5. What topics of sociological research would you be interested in and why?

CHAPTER THREE: Culture

Argot: The jargon, slang, or specialized language used by members within a group or subculture.

Counterculture: A small group that purposefully strives to challenge and eliminate key social conventions or convictions (deemed offensive by members) of a larger cultural body.

Cultural Diffusion: Associated with Everett Rogers (American, 1931–2004), sociological diffusion is the process by which a cultural idea spreads from one group to another, often through diverse avenues.

Cultural Imperialism: When a people group compels a weaker, non-dominant group to adopt or accept aspects of the dominant culture.

Cultural Leveling: The homogenization or unifying of two or more separate cultures into one equivalent social culture.

Cultural Relativism: The myopic and critical appraisal of outside cultural behavior and attitudes based upon one's presumed superior cultural perspective.

Cultural Universal: A common practice or belief shared by all societies.

Culture: The totality of a social group's specific language, epistemology, material products, ethical values, and accepted behavior.

Culture Lag: A period of adjustment when a nonmaterial culture struggles to adapt to and integrate new material offerings made available worldwide.

Culture Shock: An emotional state of disorientation, uncertainty, and apprehension that some people experience when they encounter unfamiliar cultural practices, internationally or locally.

Culture War: A sociological conflict between two or more groups over acceptable and prohibited beliefs, behaviors, or philosophies of life.

Discovery: The introduction of a unique sociological understanding of reality that brings about alternative learning opportunities, perspectives, and behavioral norms in society.

Dominant Ideology: A set of cultural beliefs and practices that legitimates existing powerful social, economic, and political interests of most people in society.

Ethnocentrism: The conclusion that one's own culture, lifestyle, and ethnic priorities are superior to all others and should epitomize the norm for all other societies.

Folkways: Norms governing everyday social behaviors and aesthetics, whose violation raise comparatively little concern.

Formal Norm: A norm that generally has been officially established, with cultural parameters beyond which brings sanctions and punishments for violators.

Guilt: A negative judgment that people make of themselves based upon a behavior or belief that they regret.

Informal Norm: A norm that is generally perceived and accepted but loosely and informally articulated or described.

High Culture: A form of culture typically associated with an elite, rich, or dominant culture.

Innovation: Contrary to an invention, an innovation refers to an alteration or addition made to an existing product or process that improves its usefulness in culture.

Invention: The creation of a device or cultural item/artifact that is new, beneficial, and recognized as a product of skill and/or genius.

Language: A system of shared symbols communicating a message comprised of speech, written characters, numbers, and nonverbal gestures and expressions.

Laws: Formal norms enforced by the state.

Material Culture: The physical resources (technology, tools, goods, cars, products, buildings, etc.) that people use to both define and support their culture.

Mores: Attitudes, conventions, or norms deemed ethically proper and beneficial to the welfare of a society or culture.

Non-material Culture: In some cultures, the act or prioritization of nonmaterial objects, abstract ideas, and intangible products such as beliefs, expressions, social rules, ideas, and language in daily existence.

Nonverbal Communication: The use of gestures, facial expressions, and other visual images to communicate.

Norm: A fixed standard (or patterns of behavior) established and maintained in society, collectively.

Popular Culture: A form of cultural expression normally associated with the masses and consumerism.

Sanction: Generally, a sanction penalty for illicit behavior concerning a social norm.

Sapir-Whorf Hypothesis: Originated by Edward Sapir (American, 1884–1939) and then further developed by Benjamin Whorf (American, 1897–1941), the idea that the language a person uses shapes his or her perception of reality and therefore his or her thoughts and actions.

Shame: An intrinsic, emotionally painful or humiliating sense of self felt when others disapprove of one's actions or beliefs.

Society: The structure of relationships within which culture is created and shared through commonly agreed upon patterns of social interaction.

Sociobiology: The systematic, scientific study of how biological forces in nature affect human social behavior.

Subculture: A small social group with unique social priorities, folkways, and moral beliefs that differs significantly from the larger cultural body surrounding it.

Taboos: Social behaviors and customs (and sometimes beliefs) that are traditionally, publicly, or institutionally forbidden, typically carrying with them a social stigma.

Technology: Centering on industry, technology includes the advancements of machinery, sophisticated engineering processes, and the utilization of material resources to provide better social comforts and conveniences in human existence.

Value: A group or individual presupposition regarding what is socially important, desirable, proper, or useful in culture.

Discussion Questions

1. Culturally, how do the "cool" people dress and act in your community? Why is it considered to be "cool" compared to others?
2. What are the differences between values, norms, and mores?
3. Describe a time in your life when you experienced "culture shock."
4. What are some of the different sub-cultures that you remember from high school?
5. What elements of culture can you perceive in operation at your college or university right now?

CHAPTER FOUR: Socialization

Anticipatory Socialization: A productive process of socialization in which a person adopts the group values and behavioral codes of a specific group that s/he wishes to join, thereby effectively rehearsing for any social position, role, or relationship that will emerge in his or her future.

Backstage Behavior: What people do when they believe that no one is observing them.

Cognitive Theory of Development: The theory of Jean Piaget (Swiss, 1896–1980) suggesting that children progress through four stages of cognitive development—the first being the sensorimotor state, wherein children learn about the world mostly through their senses and handling of objects; the second being the preoperational stage, wherein children's memory and imagination are activated; the third being the concrete operational stage, wherein children increase their sympathetic understanding and feelings for others; and the fourth being the formal operation stage, wherein children utilize logic and observation to analyze the world around them and to make future plans.

Cooperation: This social interaction occurs when people act together to promote common interests or to achieve shared goals.

Competition: A form of social conflict in which individuals or groups confine or direct the disagreement through agreed-upon rules.

Conflict: This social interaction occurs when people or groups have incompatible values, and/or when social rewards and resources are limited.

Degradation Ceremony: An aspect of the socialization process within some social institutions, in which people are subjected to humiliating, shaming rituals before sanctions or expulsion is enforced.

Exchange: Mostly self-serving, this social interaction occurs when people do something for other people with the expressed purpose of receiving a reward or return.

Face-work: The efforts that people make in social settings to present and maintain a positive, personal image to those around them, and to avoid public embarrassment for potential behavioral or belief violations.

Frontstage Behavior: What people do when they perceive that people are observing them.

Generalized Other: Introduced by George H. Mead (American, 1863–1931), the "Generalized Other" includes any norms, perspectives, and obligations in society that a person imagines will be expected of him/her within the group to which s/he belongs.

Humor: A comical reality (conventional or not) that arises from contradiction, ambiguity, and double meanings, allowing an expression of opinion without seriousness or injury.

The I: Formulated by George H. Mead (American, 1863–1931), the "I" is the socialized, subjective part of the "Self" that sponsors/directs creative, imaginative, and whimsical activities/attitudes in life.

Impression Management: The intentional (or unintentional) altered presentation of "The Self" done to manufacture a specific appearance or attitude in order to please or attract observers.

Life Course Approach: A research orientation in which sociologists and other social scientists look closely at the social factors that influence people throughout their lives, from birth to death.

Looking-Glass Self: Initiated by Charles H. Cooley (American, 1864–1929), the "Looking-Glass Self" is a concept that others represent a mirror in which people can see themselves; therefore, self-image comes from supposition and not direct, personal contemplation.

Master Status: Coined by Everett Hughes in the 1940's, "Master Status" is the position that dominates or floods out all other statuses or aspects of a person's identity.

The Me: Formulated by George H. Mead (American, 1863–1931), the "Me" is the socialized, objective part of the "Self" that judges personal behavior and performances based on how other people perceive and receive a person (in comparison or contrast).

Media: Any social avenue or establishment that spreads public information on a mass scale or communication.

Micro-Interactionism: Social interactions of this sort are more nuanced, fluid, unscripted, and individualized, with people relying more on improvisation and instinct in their responses to others.

Midlife Crisis: A stressful period of self-evaluation that begins around age forty for many people (especially for men, statistically) in Western society.

The Mind: Formulated by George H. Mead (American, 1863–1931), the "Mind" is more than just a biological organ; it is a social product and force in human existence.

Peer Group: An informal-yet-connected association of people that helps individuals develop social relationships, establishes and supports personal identities, and promotes a social agenda.

Personality: Those unique characteristics in human identities that sets individual people apart from each other.

Personal Space: The area surrounding a person that is identified and enforced (consciously or unconsciously) to convey meaning.

Resocialization: The intrinsic (or extrinsic) purposeful abandonment of older, established social attitudes or behaviors, which are replaced with new social norms, values, and activities more fitting and beneficial to one's social environment.

Rite of Passage: A symbolic ritual or ceremony that celebrates significant social and physical transitions in people's lives such as birthdays, baptisms, adulthood, weddings, funerals, etc.

Role Taking: The sociological, empathetic process of mentally assuming the perspective of another person regarding his or her attitudes or actions, and then responding from that imagined viewpoint.

Sandwich Generation: The generation of adults who simultaneously try to meet the competing needs of their parents and their children.

School: Provides new, expanding range of knowledge and skills for children, both enlarging and empowering their social world.

Self: The aspect of personality constructed from a person's self-awareness and self-image.

Significant Other: Although popularly used to identify a romantic interest, sociologically the term refers to an individual in another person's life who brings great influence, approval, and attachment.

Social Self: Formulated by George H. Mead (American, 1863–1931), the "Social Self" is comprised of three personal elements: the I, the Me, and the Mind.

Social Status: Any social position that a person holds at work, home, school, etc. or within a large group or society (such as boss, father, secretary, DJ, friend, criminal, etc.).

Symbol: Specific gestures, objects, or words utilized in human communication and understanding concerning social aesthetics, beliefs, or structural tenets.

Tact: A sensitive response to another person's activities that avoids social embarrassment and helps maintain good relations between people.

Total Institution: An establishment that controls all aspects of people's lives under a single authority, such as a prison, a school, a branch of the military, or a convent/monastery.

Discussion Questions

1. What does it mean to be a good father, socially? A good mother? A good daughter? A good son?
2. Who are you in terms of your status and roles in society right now? Do you think it will ever change? How?
3. Describe a situation or time when you used "front-stage" and "back-stage" behaviors.
4. What are the differences between the four types of social interactions: Competition, Conflict, Cooperation, and Exchange?
5. What makes a joke funny? What sociological forces do jokes play upon in society?

CHAPTER FIVE: Social Structure

Agrarian Society: The designation for a society focused primarily and economically upon agricultural business and management, with its people deeply involved in the planting, cultivation, and harvesting of crops and farmland for economic survival.

Alienation: Associated with Karl Marx (German, 1864–1920), this term describes the sorrowful state associated with capitalism and its effects upon the Proletariat (production workers) who feel isolated, dehumanized, and depressed because of their work environment.

Avatar: An online, illustrated icon or characterization of a person normally as a 2-D or 3-D image.

Bureaucracy: According to Max Weber (German, 1864–1920), a term for the most organized and efficient form of government that utilizes hierarchies and systematic regulations to maintain and promote order and efficiency.

Coalition: A continuing or nonpermanent association or partnership focused on achieving common goals.

Gemeinschaft: Associated with Ferdinand Tonnies (German, 1855–1936), this term refers to an intimate, rural community, in which unity is achieved through traditional social behaviors and rules.

Gesellschaft: Associated with Ferdinand Tonnies (German, 1855–1936), this term refers to an impersonal, urban community, coldly driven by bureaucracies and large organization, who seek to eliminate traditional bonds and relationships for economic or political efficiency and goals.

Goal Displacement: Associated with Robert Michels (German-Italian, 1876–1936), this designation refers to the bureaucratic attempts of the leadership in a large organization to replace subordinate worker goals with those more in the interests of the upper hierarchy.

Group: A broad definition for a number of people, typically with shared interests, beliefs and goals, who regularly interact with each other.

Horticultural Society: A pre-industrial, agrarian society in which people planted, cultivated, and harvested crops rather than relying upon a day-to-day collection of wild fruits and vegetables for subsistence.

Human Relations Management Theory: Associated with Elton Mayo (Australian, 1880–1949), this is a holistic approach to employee management that rests on the idea that good, effective company employees are cultivated and influenced by several factors including financial reward, beneficial work relationships, personal achievement and pride, and institutional appreciation and praise.

Hunting-and-Gathering Society: A prehistoric group of people who relied upon hunting, fishing, and collecting wild fruits and vegetables for daily subsistence.

Ideal Type: Associated with Max Weber (German, 1864–1920), the principle that all social sciences depend upon typological concepts based on theoretical, speculative scholarly ideas.

Industrial society: This term describes a type of society that prioritizes and utilizes advancing technology and mechanization to support, drive, and benefit members of the community.

In-group: This term refers to one's personal and psychological designation regarding a group of people of whom that person does identify or feel to belong.

Iron Law of Oligarchy: Associated with Robert Michels (German-Italian, 1876–1936), this theory suggests that any organization or institution, even one Democratically-run, will eventually transform into an oligarchy, wherein a small group of people maintain primary power and control.

Marriage: This term refers to the legal and continuing social relationship between two people (historically, a man and a woman) based on love, economics, and biological reproduction.

McDonaldization: A socio-economic term created by George Ritzer (American, b. 1940) suggesting that, in latter-modernity and postmodernity, everyday social interactions have come to resemble and demonstrate the structure and obtuse, perfunctory interactions of fast-food restaurants like McDonalds.

Mechanical Solidarity: Developed by Émile Durkheim (French, 1858–1917), this designation refers to the unity felt between workers because of their common vocational fields, duties, training, education, and subcultures.

Organic Solidarity: Developed by Émile Durkheim (French, 1858–1917), this designation refers to the interdependent, cooperative relationship experienced between workers in industrial countries because of their specializations and the production dependencies between each other.

Out-group: This term refers to one's personal and psychological designation regarding a group of people of whom that person does not identify nor feel to belong.

Peter Principle: Developed by Laurence J. Peter (Canadian, 1919–1990), this designation refers to the upward social movement of employees based on their positional abilities, within a bureaucracy, until they reach a vocational level wherein they are poorly-skilled or incompetent.

Plato: One of the first investigators and philosophers to focus on the structural forces of human society, Plato (Greek, 427–347 BCE) was a pupil of Socrates (Greek, one of the most important philosophers in Western society) and founded *The Academy* at Athens, which was operational until 529 CE.

Post-industrial Society: A designation for a post-industrialized society that has shifted its focus away from the production of goods and onto technology and its control or distribution.

Postmodern Society: This term refers to a larger community of people—typically young, progressive, and globalized—who collectively embrace the notions that there are no objective or absolute truths, that celebrates aesthetics and interconnectedness, and that individual choice and preferences matter more than rules and logic (which are presumed to be situational and relative).

Primary Group: This is a term used to describe a supportive, intimate group of people who live and operate daily in close contact with each other (such as a family, childhood buddies, or long-term sports teammates), cooperating and engaging in shared activities and goals.

Reference Group: This term refers to a group of people that are used as a comparison for another person to help determine proper behavior and beliefs, social norms, and social status.

Role Conflict: This situation occurs when a person in two or more social roles feels pulled in different directions due to the conflicting expectations and demands between those positions.

Role Exit: This situation occurs when people discontinue, escape, or abandon roles formerly central to their identity and set up or embrace new roles for themselves on the path for a new identity in society.

Role Strain: This situation occurs when people feel tension or stress because of required or expected demands within a single social role that are in conflict or compete with each other.

Scientific Management Approach: Also known as "Taylorism" for its originator, Frederick Taylor (American, 1856–1915), this management theory focuses on the analysis of workflow for the improvement of economic efficiency and labor productivity.

Secondary Group: This term refers to groups of people with similar goals and interests, who work together to accomplish or celebrate them.

Social Institution: A broad collective system or social entity that cultivates, maintains, and protects an organized set of beliefs, behaviors, and activities within society, such as a university, a hospital, or the F.B.I.

Social Interaction: The ways in which people attend and respond to one another in groups of two or more people.

Social Network: A collectively-driven relationship between numerous people whose contact with others links more and more people together, directly and indirectly, within the group.

Social Role: The term for the assorted behaviors, attitudes, obligations, and ideas attached to a person for his or her specific social position or circumstance such as being a mother, police officer, or teacher.

Social Structure: The term used to describe a collective, fixed, social reality that transcends individual actions, attitudes, or alteration.

Status: Unlike a social role, which is the expected behavior attached to a social position (what he or she does), status relates to the social position or prestige of a person compared to others (what he or she is), such as a gas station attendant verses a brain surgeon.

Trained Incapacity: This term describes the socialization of some people that limits their ability to respond outside of prescribed presumptions and conclusions, leading to obtuseness and myopia from experts and laypeople, bureaucrats and rulers, freethinkers and conformists, and revolutionaries and traditionalists.

Discussion Questions

1. Why do people need to have social controls set up in society?
2. What is the role of police in society and how can officers and police administrators violate that role?
3. Why do some people think that all social institutions are bad?
4. What are some types of social institutions in America? Which one is the most important? Why?
5. What is the difference between Gemeinschaft and Gesellschaft? Which one did you grow up in?

CHAPTER SIX: Deviance and Crime

Absolutist Approach: A sociological approach to social problems that assumes that a specific condition in society alone caused a specific social problem.

Beliefs: In society, people's definitions and explanations about what is assumed to be true regarding important matters such as religion, the environment, parenting, and personal rights.

Conformity: A person's internal or external alteration and modification of beliefs or behaviors resembling those of a respected peer group in order to achieve their integration and approval.

Control Theory: A theory suggesting that people's social compliance to accepted norms occurs because of internal regulation (self-control) and external motivation (peer approval or avoidance of social sanctions).

Crime: A term implying a violation of law that is unlawful, deviant, and deserving formal punitive penalties (such as the murder of an innocent child or robbing a bank), which is maintained by a governmental authority.

Criminology: The study of illegal aberrant behavior—how deviant acts become criminal, when unlawful behaviors become decriminalized, and how laws impact or influence human behavior.

Cultural Transmission: Also known as "Cultural Learning," the term used to describe how people in society pass on information or learn from others through teaching, modeling, or communication (direct or indirect).

Cyber Crime: A crime committed using a computer and/or the internet to steal data or information for financial gain. This includes installing a virus or email "bomb," illegally hacking into a computer system and/or network, or holding a computer "hostage" via a malicious computer program.

Deviance: The term used to describe a person's actions or attitudes that violate accepted, "normal" standards of behavior, which can have a negative or positive connotation or significance.

Differential Association: Associated with Edwin Sutherland (American, 1883–1950), this theory of deviance holds that people learn how and why to become criminals (the rationale, attitudes, methodology, etc.) through direct and frequent interaction with other criminals.

Differential Justice: Differences in the way that social control (through the enforcement of laws and regulations) is exercised over different groups of people depending upon factors such as race, ethnicity, economics, and gender.

Felony: A serious crime or offense that is punishable by imprisonment for longer than a year in a state prison or possibly punishable by execution.

Formal Social Control: An official, direct form of social control or forced conformity that is regulated and maintained through the institutional enforcement of laws, rules, and regulations to prevent criminal or anarchistic behaviors in society.

Hate Crime: A criminal act against a person or group of people specifically motivated by bias regarding their race, religion, gender, ethnicity, or culture.

Homicide: Succinctly, this is the illegal taking of another's life, which can be first-degree murder (premeditated), second-degree murder (an act of passion), felonious murder (killing someone while committing a different felony), voluntary manslaughter (the intentional killing without malice aforethought), and involuntary manslaughter (the unintentional killing during a non-felonious crime).

Index Crime: There are eight types of crime reported annually by the FBI in the Uniform Crime Reports that include murder, various types of rape, robbery, aggravated assault, burglary, larceny-theft, motor vehicle theft, and arson.

Informal Social Control: A casual, indirect form of social control or subtle conformity that is achieved through peer pressure, impromptu criticism of strangers to behaviors, and public emotional responses of approval (laughter or smiles) or disapproval (ridicule or mockery).

Labeling Theory: Associated with Howard Beckner (American, b. 1928), this is an approach to deviance that suggests that being labeled as "deviant" leads a person to embrace and continue with that specific deviant behavior.

Larceny: Crimes that involve grand or petty theft (depending upon the value of the goods), burglary (unlawful entry), robbery (personal theft), embezzlement, fraud, or extortion (blackmail).

Law: A system of governmental decrees (Federal, State, Municipal) that set and maintain national and local social standards for public (and sometimes private) behavior, the breaking of which will incur penalties (felonies, misdemeanors, fines) for the transgressor.

Medical Model: An antiquated theory suggesting that social problems are linked to "bad people" who have a mental deficiency or disorder, lack proper education, or have received incomplete socialization.

Misdemeanor: A less serious crime or offense that is punishable by a just fine or possibly imprisonment in a local or county jail for less than a year.

Obedience: Volitional or forced acquiescence to the rules or requests of another person, group, or hierarchical governmental organization.

Organized Crime: An association or cartel of professional criminals (also known as "Gangsters" or "Mobsters"), often operating at an international level, who utilize widespread secretive, illegal, and illicit activities (such as selling drugs, prostitution, gambling) to fund and propel their nefarious enterprise to greater profits and cultural power in the criminal world. Examples include the Italian Mafia, various Central and South American drug cartels, the Japanese Yakuza, and the Russian Mafia (also known as "Bratva").

Sanction: A public punitive action dispensed upon a person or group for behavior or attitudes that violate an accepted social norm.

Social Control: The term for the formal and informal socialization implemented to cultivate acceptable social behaviors and to inhibit deviant, detrimental behaviors in society.

Social Disorganization Theory: The theory suggesting that high crime rates and criminality are directly related to neighborhood ecological and environmental factors. In other words, where a person lives is more influential in whether he or she becomes involved in illegal pursuits than individual traits like race, gender, or age.

Societal-Reaction Approach: Part of symbolic interactionism, this is another term for labeling theory, which suggests that one's identity is derived from the names and descriptions (labels) that others apply to the person because of his or her deviant behavior.

Strain Theory: This theory suggests that deviance occurs when a gap exists between cultural goals and achievements. To achieve these goals, a person accepts the goals but uses illegal methods to achieve them (Innovation); a person rejects the goals but uses legitimate methods to achieve them (Ritualism); a person rejects both the goals and legitimate methods of achieving them (Retreatism); or a person rejects the goals and legitimate methods of achievement, creating new goals and new methods of achieving them (Rebellion).

Stigma: A label, term, or classification given to a person or group that devalues and brings disgrace, often leading to social exclusion.

Transnational Crime: A violation of the law by agents from multiple countries who plan, carryout, and risk negative legal repercussions, internationally, because of the infraction.

Values: Social agreements within various groups regarding ideas, attitudes, and actions considered to be good or bad, helpful or destruction, and moral or dishonorable.

Victimization Survey: A questionnaire or interview given to a sample of the population to determine whether people have been victims of crime.

Victimless Crime: The term used to describe illicit, illegal activities (such as prostitution or gambling) consensually committed between people that causes no overt harm or damage to the perpetrators.

White-collar Crime: The term used to describe unlawful, non-violent activities (for financial gain and corporate advantage) often perpetrated by respected business men and women, which includes embezzlement, bribery, insider trading, money laundering, etc.

Discussion Questions

1. What is the difference between deviance and crime?
2. Is being deviant always wrong? When could it be correct, socially?
3. Some people shrug off violations of the law saying, "It's just a misdemeanor." Is this a helpful attitude to have in society? Why?
4. What are the differences between the different levels of homicide?
5. What social functions do prisons and jails hold in society?

CHAPTER SEVEN: Social Class

Absolute Poverty: The lowest level of existence regarding basic human necessities like food, water, housing, proper sewage disposal, beneath which a person cannot survive.

Achieved Status: Attributed to Ralph Linton (American, 1893–1953), this term refers to the meritorious social status that a person creates for him or herself in deeds, character, or skillfulness.

Addams, Jane: Nicknamed the "mother of social work" and the first American to ever received the *Nobel Peace Prize* (1931), Addams (American, 1860–1935) was a sociologist, political activist, reformer, and social worker in Chicago, Illinois (and later throughout the United States).

Ascribed Status: Much like a "Caste System," this designation refers to the social status that a person receives or is assigned at birth (or unwillingly later on in life) that restricts or improves their prestige in society.

Bolsheviks: The small faction of Marxist Social Democrats under the leadership of Vladamir "Lenin" Ulianov (Russian, 1870–1924) who were dedicated to the destruction of the capitalist system in place in Tsarist Russian in the early twentieth century.

Bourgeoisie: The term that Karl Marx (German, 1818–1883) assigned to the middle class in the capitalist system, whom he claimed to monopolize and dominate culture and/or the government at the expense of the proletariat (or working class).

Capitalism: An economic system utilized in industrial societies to increase personal profits through an economic climate of free competition, laissez-faire governmental control, private ownership of property, a pursuit of maximum profit.

Caste System: A rigid, inescapable, inherited social class (especially in India and other Hindu cultures), that suppresses personal freedoms and social prestige.

Class: A term used to describe the economic level or standing of a group of people within a society.

Class Consciousness: Associated with Marxism, this designation refers to the subjective (and often self-serving presumptions) by fellow class constituents or members regarding their economic standing, system, interests, and goals to bring about social changes, if needed.

Class System: An overarching social order, which can be fixed or fluid (depending upon the culture and historical era) that focuses on people's economic level or prestige within a society.

Closed System: A suppressive social order, with little to no room for social mobility for specific people groups, that focuses on people's economic level or ascribed status within a society.

Cultural Capital: Associated with Pierre Bourdieu (French, 1930–2002), this designation refers to the amassing of knowledge, linguistic skills, cultural adroitness, and behaviors that indicate one's social standing or prestige (or a lack therein).

Digital Divide: The vast differences or gulf between high-income and low-income groups in relation to their technological access (communication, computer, internet, etc.).

Dominant Ideology: Associated with Karl Marx (German, 1818–1883), this designation refers to the culture, accepted social behaviors, political philosophy, and economic practices of the majority group within a society.

Estate System: Also known as feudalism, this is a controversial term used to describe the political organization and system in the Middle Ages (roughly, 500–1500 CE) wherein an elite member of society (a.k.a., a "lord") wielded social power and control over a group of people (a.k.a., "vassals"), who agreed to do agricultural (and other work) for the lord in exchange for protection and land, although the details of this exchange varied from country to country.

Esteem: In public, the favorable reputation or respect given to a person within an occupation or activity; privately (i.e., self-esteem), one's personal, subjective, often emotional assessment of his/her own worthiness in society.

False Consciousness: Associated with Marxism, this designation refers to the unconscious apathy and social acquiescence that the working class (a.k.a., the Proletariat) demonstrate regarding their dreadful economic/social environment and their exploitative economic rulers (a.k.a., the Bourgeoisie).

Horizontal Mobility: The ability of a person or group to move in social or economic standing within (and not above or below) a specific rank or status.

Income: An economic, aggregate summary of all the money and wages that a person holds at a given time (such as an hour, month, or year).

Intergenerational Mobility: The ability of a person or group to change his or her social or economic standing relative to his or her parents' own social or economic rank.

Intragenerational Mobility: The ability of a person or group to move in social or economic standing within that person's own lifetime.

Life Chances: Advanced by Max Weber (German, 1864–1920), this designation refers to the opportunities and possibilities of people in a society to improve upon their wealth, income, living conditions, and social status.

Marx, Karl: Few individuals have been as influential or socially impactful in world history as the historian, philosopher, journalist, and social scientist Karl Marx (German, 1818–1883), the co-author of *The Communist Manifesto* (1848).

New Jim Crow: A theory advanced by Michelle Alexander (American, b. 1967) suggesting that the War on Drugs (beginning in the mid-1970s) and its accompanying incarcerations in the criminal justice system were set in place and used to create a new caste system that targeted Blacks, Hispanics, and other non-Whites in America.

Open System: A fluid social order, with multiple opportunities for social mobility for specific people groups, that focuses on people's economic level or achieved status within a society.

Party: Advanced by Max Weber (German, 1864–1920), this term refers a group of people in society who are organized to accomplish a political goal.

Prestige: A term used to describe a person's social standing, respect, and or influence in greater society.

Proletariat: The term that Karl Marx (German, 1818–1883) assigned to the working class in the capitalist system, whom he claimed would rise up and revolt against the bourgeoisie (or middle class), who had oppressed them for centuries.

Relative Poverty: A fluid economic condition wherein a person or people-group lives below the average economic standards of their own society.

Slavery: An economic, political, total state or system of servitude wherein people are considered property and therefore can be owned by other people.

Social Inequality: Individually or collectively, this designation is used to describe a social state in which some members of society have greater or lesser amounts of income, wealth, social prestige, or political power.

Social Mobility: The ability of a person or group to move in social or economic standing from one rank to another (up or down).

Socio-Economic Status (SES): Similar to the notion of wealth, this is a designation used to describe a person's aggregate social and economic measure based on his or her income, education level, occupation, and social standing.

Status Group: According to Max Weber (German, 1864–1920), this designation describes a group of people in society who are called out from other people or groups based on their social standing, culture, ethnicity, religion, or race.

Stratification: The hierarchical ranking of all people-groups within a society that displays economic division and power along with political and social dominance (or weakness).

Underclass: Originally associated with Gunnar Myrdal (Swedish, 1898–1987), this term refers to the poorest and socially weakest group of people in a class hierarchy, whose social standing restricts or prevents social benefits or upward mobility.

Vertical Mobility: The ability of a person or group to rise in social or economic standing from a lower rank or status.

Wealth: An economic, aggregate summary of all the money, savings, land, investments, and material resources that a person holds at a given time.

Discussion Questions

1. What is your ascribed status? What is your achieved status?
2. Did your family associate with families from other social classes? Did you notice it when you were a child?
3. Are you cognizant of your socioeconomic class right now? How does that make you feel?
4. In order to be rich, do people have to steal from or oppress the poor? Why?
5. Describe a time when you feel like you had social capital.

CHAPTER EIGHT: Global Inequality

Banana Republic: A term for smaller countries in Central and South America whose economic prosperity depends upon the cultivation, harvesting, and sale of one main crop for exportation into foreign countries.

Borderlands: The region of common culture along national borders such as between Mexico and the United States.

Colonialism: Historically, colonialism is the establishment of a group of settlers in a foreign land with the expressed goal of a permanent settlement, regional and political hegemony (but not necessarily harmony), and the exploitation of resources and people for economic gain in the colony and for the mother country.

Core Countries: A term denoting countries with advanced technology and industry upon which many underdeveloped countries depend, economically.

Dependency Theory: Associated with Andre G. Frank (German, 1929–2005), the theory that formerly colonized countries experience global inequality because of their previous exploitation by Western powers such as England and France, who extracted materials and monopolized human labor from these colonized countries, leaving their former colonial lands dependent upon the Western countries for the products of first-world industrialization.

Feminization of Poverty: The argument that women suffer the most in impoverished nations because they are paid less than men in most wage-paying jobs, they have far less education than men of the same age, they own less land and income-generating equipment, and are more likely to be saddled with child-rearing duties, all of which restricts their economic opportunities and rewards.

Global Inequality: Focuses mostly upon income differences (and the power that brings or is lacking) between the countries of the world.

Globalization: The increased exchange of trade, people, investments, technology, customs, ideas, and values between foreign countries (originally pushed along via Imperialism and Western empire-building), which affects all countries economically, culturally, and politically.

Gross National Product (GNP): The yearly aggregate financial worth of a nation's goods and services, which is determined by adding the gross domestic product value and the net income from foreign financing, together.

Human Development Index (HDI): A listing or measure of a combination of factors to determine one's economic state based on life expectancy, per capita income, and total years in the educational system (including adulthood).

Human Rights: The idea that all human beings deserve basic moral entitlements and freedoms (such as the right to life, legal equality, freedom of expression or speech, etc.) regardless of age, race, religion, gender, or nationality, and which cannot be taken away or conditionally provided by any governmental body.

Market-Oriented Theories: These theories suggest that a laissez-faire style of government, with its promotion and permission of individual economic freedom, will benefit countries, ultimately.

Migradollars: A term for the monies or funds that immigrants earn in their adopted countries (such as the United States) but are returned to their families of origin in their native land (especially in Mexico).

Modernization: The far-reaching process by which nations pass from traditional forms of social organization toward those characteristic of post–Industrial Revolution societies.

Modernization Theory: This theory suggests that poorer countries and societies will benefit economically if they abandon their traditional business methods and replace them with advanced technology, progressive cultural values, and modern entrepreneurial strategies.

Multinational Corporation: A commercial organization with headquarters in one country, but who manages and develops business activities in several different countries across the globe, simultaneously.

Neocolonialism: The economic custom that utilizes capitalism and increases globalization through cultural imperialism in order to develop a continuing dependence of a colony (and its native lands) on a foreign, distant-yet-dominant country.

Neoliberalism: An approach to economic growth that rests on the idea that laissez-faire economic governmental policies boost economic growth.

Newly Industrialized Economies (NIE): A term to describe 2nd world countries who have embraced advanced technology and industry, and who are experiencing a rise in economic growth and dominance.

Refugees: Historically, the people groups who left their native countries and entered nearby foreign lands because of warfare, natural disasters, or political oppression.

Remittances: A term for the monies or funds that immigrants earn in their adopted countries and return to their families of origin in their native lands.

Third World Countries: Although originally coined during the Cold War period to label the various countries who chose to align with neither the NATO (Western) countries or the Communist Bloc (Eastern), currently the term refers to several developing, more impoverished countries in Africa, Asia, and South America.

World Systems Analysis: Associated with Immanuel Wallerstein (American, b. 1930) who views the global economic system as one divided between key industrialized nations that control wealth and the weaker developing countries that can be controlled and their resources exploited.

Discussion Questions

1. How do the three types of poverty differ?
2. What social or cultural factors or forces cause poverty?
3. What social problems are caused by inequality?
4. How does poverty in America differ from poverty in India?
5. Is it hard for a poor person to become rich in America? Explain.

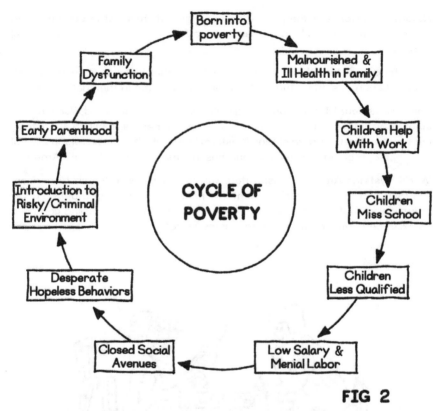

FIG 2

Figure 2: Cycle of Poverty
Source: John Knox and Daniel Schallau.

CHAPTER NINE: Gender and Age

Activity Theory: Associated with Robert Havighurst (American, 1900–1991), this theory of aging implicitly suggests that elderly people who remain socially active and engaged will be socially, psychologically, and physically healthier than those who retreat from society.

Ageism: A term referring to and discrimination expressed and experienced based on a person's age (old or young).

Age Discrimination: Unjust, prejudicial conduct toward people because of their age (young or old).

Ageists: People who avoid the elderly on an individual level, who discriminate against them regarding employment, who deride them and their physical condition through mockery, and who judge them to be a drain on social resources—thus needing to be removed from society than their gender opposites.

Complementarian Leadership: Typically a religious notion, complementarianism suggests that men and women have natural traits that make them better suited for gender-specific duties and roles in society than their gender opposites.

Disengagement Theory: Associated with Elaine Cumming (North America) and Warren E. Henry (North America), this highly criticized theory of aging (due to a lack of empirical support) suggests that the elderly naturally and volitionally withdraw from society because of their loss of personal and physical abilities, and that this disengagement is accepted by others within their social environments.

Expressive Leader: A person in a family (father, mother, or child) who accepts responsibility for seeing that harmonious relationships within and outside the family unit are maintained, cultivated, and preserved.

Feminism: Historically divided into three time periods—called "Waves"—in modernity (the nineteenth and early twentieth centuries, the 1960s–1980s, and the 1990s–2000s), this international social movement sought/seeks to improve living and working conditions for women throughout the world regarding social, economic, and political equality for women.

Gender: Rather than biologically determined, gender refers to the different (and fluid) cultural concepts that men and women perform or display in society.

Gender Roles: Refers to cultural positions (with their relative behaviors, attitudes, and duties) that are typically expected of men and women in society.

Gender Role Socialization: Refers to the traditional gender socialization from parents, school, peers, and mass media regarding what it means to be a man or woman in society.

Gender Stratification: The presumption that men and women have unequal access to social power, standing, and resources because of their biological sex.

Gerontology: The study of the sociological and psychological aspects of aging and the problems of the aged that utilizes psychology, anthropology, physical education, counseling, and medicine.

Glass Ceiling: A political and purposeful obstacle that prevents or hampers the social and financial rise of qualified individuals at their workplace because of their gender, race, religion, or ethnicity.

Homophobia: Unlike a moral or religious objection to the LGBTQ community, homophobia is an emotional or psychological state wherein people embrace and display unreasonable fears, prejudice, negative attitudes, and bigotry against homosexual people and their sexual lifestyle.

Homosexuality: A term to define people who are sexually-attracted to members of their own sex, which historically has been a departure from social, scientific, religious, and moral norms, but who have experienced greater social and political acceptance in postmodernity.

Hospice Care: Treatment of the terminally ill in their own homes, or in special hospital units or other facilities, with the goal of helping them to die comfortably, without pain.

Institutional Discrimination: An established and organized pattern of manage-ment that systematically denies a minority group access to economic resources and opportunities as part of society's normal functionality.

Instrumental Leader: A person in a family (father, mother, or child) who accepts responsibility for seeing that family tasks are completed and that family goals are pursued while simultaneously managing relationships within and outside the family unit.

Martineau, Harriet: A brilliant scholar, essayist, novelist, and journalist during the Victorian Era (1837–1901 CE), Martineau (British, 1802–1876) is considered to be the first female sociologist in Western society.

Multiple Masculinities: Tied closely to Raewyn Connell (Australian, b. 1944) and her theory of gender order, multiple masculinities is the idea that men from all societies are provided opportunities to learn and experience a full range of gender roles and activities outside of traditional avenues, across cultures, and throughout history.

Second Shift: This term refers to the increased weekly workload (the combination of outside employment and domestic duties at home) that women do compared to men, who limit their labor to their jobs outside the home.

Sex: Tied to natural biological traits, the term, "sex," refers to the thousands of scientific differences between human males and females.

Sex Typing: Somewhat fluid internationally and inter-culturally, this refers to the association of some activities or jobs to be either "male" or "female" such as childcare or construction.

Sexism: The practice or philosophy of men or women that suggests that one's biological sex group is superior and the opposite group is inferior.

Split Labor Market: An economic division wherein a primary labor market is reserved for elites (people who will advance to high-level positions) and a poorly-paying secondary labor market with little to no job security or mobility.

XX Chromosomes: The scientific, genetic marker indicating a human female.

XY Chromosomes: The scientific, genetic marker indicating a human male.

Discussion Questions

1. Why do the elderly need the young, and the young need the elderly?
2. What scares you most about growing old? Why?
3. It has been said that boys are more destructive than girls when they play with toys. If true, is this because of their biological natures or because of parental nurturing and socialization? Defend your position.
4. What are some common expectations regarding how men and women should behave and dress?
5. What are the differences between an instrumental leader and an expressive leader? Which one would you like to be? Why?

CHAPTER TEN: Race and Ethnicity

Affirmative Action: Also known as "positive discrimination," this is the governmental or institutional policy of providing preferential treatment (greater facilitation of opportunities for education, employment, economic aid, etc.) to minority and underrepresented groups in an attempt to cultivate a more egalitarian workplace or educational community.

Amalgamation: The uniting or combining of two separate cultures (often called "The Melting Pot") to create a new, distinctive culture.

Anti-Semitism: When someone holds hateful or prejudicial positions against the Jewish people, their culture, and Judaism.

Apartheid: This term refers to the official segregation policy of the South African government (1948–1993), which sought to separate blacks and non-whites from the whites, who were in the cultural majority.

Assimilation: A slow process of sociological adoption and abandonment wherein people give up the traditional practices and beliefs of their former culture, substituting them with practices and beliefs of another culture, of which they eventually identify and become members.

Black Power: First politically utilized by Stokely Carmichael, a.k.a. Kwame Ture (Trinidadian, 1941–1998), this is the political motto for the African-American civil rights movement of the 1960s and 1970s, which advocated for racial pride, social equality, increasing cultural power, and better economic opportunities for black Americans (and people of color across the globe).

Color-blind Racism: Also known as "Aversive Racism" and associated with the notion of "white privilege," this is the (controversial) political idea that a subtle form of racism exists, which falsely asserts that race and skin color no longer are a social issue in postmodernity.

Discrimination: The practice or philosophy of depriving people or groups access to social respect, legal protections, and cultural benefits because of ascribed traits such as race, gender, ethnicity, or any other arbitrary factor.

Du Bois, W.E.B.: One of the most influential African-American political activists, Dr. Du Bois, PhD (American, 1868–1963) was a prolific writer, scholar, and journalist in post-Civil War America. Later in life, he taught at several universities in the United States and was editor of the *Niagara Movement* magazines—*The Moon* and *The Horizon*—as well as editor for the *NAACP* magazine, *The Crisis.*

Ethnic Group: A term used to delineate a group of people who associate together or who are perceived to share common characteristics such as heritage, language, clothing, religion, and unique customs.

Ethnocentrism: The practice of presuming that one's own culture—with its customs, values, and collective beliefs—are superior to all other societies' ways and represents the epitome of proper social norms.

Exploitation Theory: As promoted by Eugen von Bohm-Bawerk (Austrian, 1851–1914), this semi-Marxist theory suggests that capitalism, with its embrace and promotion of private wealth and profit-making enterprise, provides massive benefits for the elite, rich owners at the expense and exclusion of the working or slave class.

Expulsion: The planned, methodical physical relocation and/or removal of a politically weaker people group by a dominant, powerful group to a region with greater social risks, less resources, and fewer benefits.

Genocide: The systematic, large-scale extermination of an entire ethnic group or nation for political, racial, or economic reasons.

Intergroup Contact Hypothesis: Associated with Gordon Allport (American, 1897–1967), this theory suggests that personal or community prejudices in a social setting can be decreased through increased social contact and interaction between two opposing groups.

Institutional Discrimination: The systematic, organized, unfair treatment of a person or a group (whether deliberate, accidental, or unknowingly) because of their race, gender, or ethnicity, resulting in the suppression of their access to social respect, legal protections, and cultural benefits.

Minority Group: According to Louis Wirth (American, 1897–1952), minority groups are set apart by the majority group(s), and thus experience collective discrimination and unequal treatment because of their racial, ethnic, cultural, or religious identities.

Model or Ideal Minority: A term used in Sociology to delineate a minority group who has achieved great social success (economic, cultural, education) despite any previous social bigotry or discrimination.

Pluralism: In Sociology, the idea of two or more distinct people groups or cultures peacefully coexisting in society, appreciating and accepting their differences and cultural attributes, as long as all groups follow and respect the laws of the land.

Prejudice: An emotional or irrational presumption regarding a specific individual or people group, typically leading to animosity and hostile treatment toward other people of that ethnicity, gender, or religion.

Race: A term to describe a distinct people group who are differentiated from other people groups because of biological or physical features considered socially important.

Racial Formation Theory: Associated with Michael Omi (American) and Howard Winant (American, b. 1946), this theory suggests that racial designations, being more fluid than fixed, are created, transformed, or negated through a socio-economic-historical process.

Racial Profiling: Often condemned for its use by police to target non-white people for potential illegal activities, racial profiling bases its suspicions mainly on a person's race, ethnicity, gender, age, or national origin rather than overt criminal behavior.

Racism: A term referring to the belief that one's race is the highest and greatest among all other races regarding natural abilities and cultural offerings.

Segregation: A term referring to forced, sometimes legal physical separation between groups of people, which is often based upon a person's race or ethnic identity, leading to a reduction of their rights and social benefits.

Spencer, Herbert: With a strong background in mathematics and natural science, Spencer (British, 1820–1903) was an advocate of evolutionary theory and its potential application in understanding how socities function and what drives them (also known as *Social Darwinism*).

Stereotype: A simplistic, common, unverifiable generalization or understanding (negative or positive) regarding a specific people or cultural group, such as white men cannot jump high in basketball, gay men have good fashion sense, or that Italian women have feisty tempers, etc.

Symbolic Ethnicity: A term that describes the admiration and loyalty that people sometimes profess regarding an ethnic group, cultural tradition, or practice outside of one's own ethnic identity and heritage.

Washington, Booker T.: A former slave, Washington (American, 1856–1915) was an influential educator, reformer, and social advocate for African-American civil rights after the *Reconstruction Period* (1863–1877) and the turn of the century.

White Privilege: Akin to the psychological idea of "Gaslighting" (that some people are unaware of their inherent bigotry and racism), this term refers to the social, cultural, and institutional benefits that all white people receive because of being part of the white race.

Discussion Questions

1. How do sociologists define race and ethnicity?
2. What are prejudice and discrimination? Have you ever experienced either? Explain.
3. What are some potential consequences of race and ethnicity regarding social opportunities?
4. What are some false racial and ethnic stereotypes promoted in movies and television?
5. What are some social problems that can occur by telling someone, "You do not understand because you are [insert color]"?

CHAPTER ELEVEN: Social Change

Astroturfing: The political advocacy or promotion of a specific group or political agenda that is "grassroots" in appearance only.

American Civil Rights Movement: A social rights campaign comprised of both black and white people who fought for greater Constitutional rights and protections, as well as the dismantling of institutional segregation in schools and social environs during the fifties and sixties across America (but mostly in the South).

American Revolution: The name for the American colonial revolt (1765–1783) that rose against the British Empire under King George III (British, 1738–1820), ending with political independence for the thirteen rebelling colonies and the formal establishment of the United States of America.

Asymmetical Warfare: Conflict between two parties, with groups holding greater or lesser military or national power, and who utilize significantly different strategy or tactics in their battles.

Bolshevik Revolution: Also called the October Revolution, this popular uprising occurred in Russia in 1917–1918 and concluded with the overthrow and execution of Czar Nicholas II and his entire family.

Boomarang Children: The term in postmodern culture for adult children who return to live with their parents mostly for financial reasons.

Causation: In Sociology, the influence of one or more social forces resulting in change for another factor or agent.

Chinese Cultural Revolution: Also known as the Chinese Communist Revolution, this is the name for the civil war that took place between Chiang Kai-Shek (Chinese, 1887–1975) and his Nationalist supporters and Mao Zedong (Chinese, 1893–1976) and his Communist supporters, ending with the ousting of the Chinese Nationalist Party who fled from mainline china to Taiwan, later to be called "The Republic of China," and the establishment of the Communist "Peoples Republic of China" in 1949.

Culture lag: First termed by William F. Ogburn (American, 1886–1959), this refers to the period of time it takes for some cultures to adjust to unexpected social change and technological advancements within society.

Cyclical Theory: Unlike the social progress and advancement suggested in Evolutionary Theory, this theory suggests that all societies experience periods of birth, growth, decline, and collapse.

Emergent-Norm Perspective: The influence of social norms regarding the emergence or maintenance of collective behavior.

Equilibrium Model: The view that society tends toward a state of stability or balance, with members trying to preserve a healthy balance between tasks and emotional needs.

Evolutionary Theory: In Sociology, this refers to the theory of social change suggesting that society is moving in a definite direction, normally presumed to be better, more progressive, and more advanced.

Fad: An informal, frivolous activity or behavior that is popular in general society but short-lived.

False Consciousness: With the Communist theory of Karl Marx (German, 1818–1883) in mind, this term is used to describe the erroneous attitudes and social analyses of the working class (also called the Proletariat) regarding the economic inequalities, oppression, and exploitation that surround them in capitalist society.

Fashion: A temporary clothing or aesthetic trend that eventually transforms into a long-lasting cultural element or artifact.

French Revolution: The internal, violent, political rebellion that occurred in France from 1789–1799, which ended with the termination of centuries-old monarchial control, the execution of the king and queen of France in 1793, the establishment of the French Republic in 1792, and the rule of Napoleon Bonaparte (French, 1769–1821).

Luddites: Rebellious craft workers in nineteenth-century England (ca. 1811–1816) who destroyed new factory machinery as part of their resistance during the Industrial Revolution.

New Social Movement: The informal but discernable collective pursuit of a social goal concerning cultural values and social identities, as well as pragmatic social improvements in group life.

Personal Sociology: The process of recognizing the impact one's individual position has on who people are and how they think and act, and of and taking responsibility for the impacts their actions have on others.

Participant-Oriented Movements: A term coined by sociologists Turner (American, 1920–2014) and Killian (American, 1919–2010), this is a social movement that is more about the pleasure of involvement than the social agenda promoted by a group.

Power-Oriented Movements: A term coined by sociologists Turner (American, 1920–2014) and Killian (American, 1919–2010), these social campaigns are more about the acquisition of power and status rather than the social agenda promoted by a group.

Public Sociology: The political process of bringing insights gained through sociological observation and analysis into the public or collective sphere, with the specific goal of seeking to bring about positive social change.

Relative Deprivation: The conscious feeling or perception of a negative economic reality between minority and majority groups and present actualities, often giving rise to civil unrest, protests, and movements.

Resource Mobilization Theory: This theory suggests that the success or failure of various social movements is due mostly because of the availability and utilization of money, political influence, media access, and personnel resources for certain groups, historically.

Social Change Theory: The sociological adjustments or adaptions over time regarding social structures, cultural symbols, behavior patterns, and collective norms and values.

Social Innovation: The fresh and creative use of material goods, cultural symbols, and personal resources to affect personal or collective improvement in society.

Social Movement: A loosely organized group whose activities are pursued in order to obtain or resist change regarding social structure, beliefs, and/or norms.

Social Revolution: The sudden and dramatic change in the structure of society, typically ending with a shift in social dominance for one group that displaces another, sometimes violently.

Technology: The use of products and procedures stemming from scientific knowledge and advancements to satisfy and/or improve upon social needs and wants.

Transhumanism: Associated with Max More (British, b. 1964), this postmodern theory suggests that all people can and will experience evolutionary leaps and greater human existence, physically and cognitively, through the development and utilization of future scientific and technological advancements.

Value-Oriented Movements: These social campaigns seek to affect grand social changes—institutionally and culturally.

Vested Interests: Those people or groups who will suffer (economically, politically, or physically) in the event of social change, and who have a stake in maintaining the status quo in society.

Discussion Questions

1. What are some factors that cause social change in society?
2. What sort of social changes have you experienced or observed, personally?
3. Do you feel like you have the possibility for upward or downward social mobility in your own life? Why?
4. What is the difference between a fashion and a fad? Provide examples of each.
5. What similarities and differences were there between the American, Russian, and Chinese Revolutions?

CHAPTER TWELVE: Religion

Alternative Spirituality Practices: These practices are found within the Holistic Milieu and include various extra-biblical and untraditional practices historically associated with the New Age Movement, Paganism, various hybrid-Buddhist movements, etc. Despite their untraditional or extra-biblical character, some participants still sugested a sacredness or spiritual-ness of the practices.

Atheism: This is a belief system that asserts that no god (or a pantheon of gods) exists in the universe. Many atheists base this disbelief on the persistent and historical presence of evil, the misbehavior of Christians, modern scientific thought, and radical individualism ostensibly making each human their own deity. Ultimately, according to atheists, ancient religious superstitions can be ignored (such as Christianity, Judaism, Hinduism, etc.) because intelligent, mature minds reject the notion of a supernatural world and only rely upon empirical data and personal perceptions of reality.

Autonomization: Related to privatization and the subjectivization of religion, this approach suggests that the sociological paradigm shift that has taken place in Western society inextricably involves the growing prominence of the individual in religious matters—specifically regarding the intimate, personal nature of faith; the newfound personal authority in religious doctrine and expression; and the embrace (or dismissal) of religious beliefs and adherence based upon relevancy for the individual.

Classic Sociologists of Religion: Although many scholars have contributed to the development of the sociology of religion in history, three main pioneers are highlighted: French Sociologist Émile Durkheim (1858–1917) held that all religions exhibit social "facts" because all religions are based upon interpretations of the sacred world (worldly things are called "the profane"). German philosopher and historian Karl Marx (1818–1883) suggested that religion had been used historically to control the masses, adding to the social problems of inequality and inequity in societies. Finally, German economist and sociologist Max Weber (1864–1920) asserted that, because of the dynamic, undefinable nature of religion, it could only be understood from a subjective perspective.

Congregational Domain: This is a taxological term encompassing the various sociological and religious elements found within a region or populace. It includes congregations of difference, which are predominately Protestant and affirming of personal piety in one's faith; congregations of experiential difference, which are charismatically-evangelical and open to more dramatic manifestations of spiritual activity in people's lives; congregations of humanity, which predominately include mainline liberal denominations focused on social work over spirituality; and last, congregations of experiential humanity, which focus upon the inner spiritual experience over the externals of religion such as Scripture or the Sacraments. They are mostly non-liturgical, Unitarian, or Quaker.

Emerging Church: This is a term that refers to postmodern, mostly-white congregations reaching out to seekers, non-believers, and anti-institutional Christians through creative, community-driven, individualistic expressions and understandings of faith. There is some debate to where the movement originated; some say California, USA; others say that it began in Australia or Great Britain.

Faith: This orientation of the self relates to people's internal supernatural convictions as well as their associated religious beliefs and attitudes.

Gen X: This generation was born sometime around 1965–1980, and are known for being self-sufficient and individualistic, which sometimes translates into a cynical disdain for authority (including institutional Christianity). Based on recent key sociological surveys, though, the religious loyalty of Gen X is nearly twice as high as the Baby Boomers Generation that came before them.

Gen Y: Also known as Millennials, this generation was born sometime around 1980–2000, and are much less religiously active (but not necessarily less spiritual) than previous generations, which is evidenced by their willingness to experiment with alternative spirituality practices formerly associated with paganism and the occult. Additionally, whereas their predecessors

(Gen X) were pridefully self-sufficient, Millennials are radical individualists with a higher sense of entitlement, empowerment, and emotionalism compared to other generations, based on recent key sociological surveys.

Gen Z: Also known as iGen (for the Internet), this generation was born after 1996–2000, with the end date of their era still to be determined. According to recent key sociological surveys, they are twice as likely to embrace atheism compared to previous generations, and they are more socially and religiously diverse than other previous generations.

God: In Judeo-Christian thought, God is an eternal being who created the heavens and the earth through his personal will and supernatural powers. Also, there are different understandings of what and who God is. In Scripture, God is a single being who exists simultaneously as three distinct persons (Father, Jesus, the Holy Spirit), ontologically. This "three-in-one-ness" is not just in the activities that God does; as the great Jewish prayer, the Shema, states in Deuteronomy 6:4, "Here, O Israel: The Lord your God, the Lord is one." Although the mechanics and physics of God's existence are paradoxical and mystical in many ways, what is observable from the Bible is that God is love, light, the truth, invisible (currently), immutable, all-gracious, all-just, all-merciful, and all-powerful. He is also the creator of all human beings and societies, beginning with the Adam and Eve story in the biblical book of Genesis.

The Holistic Milieu: This spiritual environment includes a belief in (and involvement with) alternative spirituality practices that participants consider spiritual in nature, a plurality in religious activity that allows for dual membership in traditional and alternative practices, a strong sense of community, and a cautionary outlook in life and relationships.

The Kendal Project: From 2000–2002, two British scholars—Paul Heelas and Linda Woodhead—undertook an in-depth study of the religiosity and spiritual practices in Kendal, England. Specifically, the research team investigated traditional religious involvement and attendance compared to alternative spiritual practices found in the more nebulous holistic milieu, concluding that many people were abandoning mainstream Christianity for non-traditional, extra-biblical activities often found in the New Age Movement or New Paganism.

Liberalism: A nineteenth-century philosophical movement begun in response to modernity its growth of scientific discoveries that pushed back against the traditionalism of earlier generations; it set forth to understand religion's relationship to the scientific world, to explain the relationship of Christianity (and other faiths) in history, and to refute the superstitions of the Old World, which many liberals believed was still being practiced and promoted by religious groups, world-wide.

Mysticism: Found in every religious tradition, historically, adherents of this movement and belief system claim to have had direct contact with God (also called theophanies), a unique supernatural perception or understanding of events leading to intense joy and a sense of perfect union with God. Some examples of mystics include Bernard of Clairvaux, Clare of Assisi, Hildegard of Bingen, Mechthild of Magdeburg, and Meister Eckhardt.

New Age Movement (NAM): People in the New Age Movement (part of the holistic milieu) express their faith more as radical individualists than communally or institutionally. Despite being anti-institutional, they are not necessarily opposed to the notion of Jesus or the use of the Bible, they are personally committed to their spiritual quests, and they appreciate and utilize non-traditional avenues of religion and spirituality in their lives.

The Nones: This postmodern people-group (mostly Gen Y or Millennials), who neither claim nor participate with any particular religious tradition, are not necessarily atheistic nor secular. Instead, they still remain interested in a spiritual side to life even though they tend to shy away from defining or codifying it, corporately.

Postmodernism: Mostly a Western-focused era that pushed backed against the dogma and tenets espoused in modernism, this period began around 1985 (or earlier) and promotes a relativistic approach to reality, religion, morals, culture, and narratives. Thus, postmodernists do not believe in absolutes or traditional understandings of history and beliefs; instead, they dismiss all central, collective narratives for a diverse, fluid, and eclectic understanding of truth that is solely personally-determined.

The Profane: According to French sociologist Émile Durkheim (1858–1917), the profane refers to all collective mundane ideas and artifacts that are part of normal social life.

Rational Choice Theory: This is a religious theory proposed in modernity, which suggests that religion flourishes in society if particular religious groups or beliefs provide participants with tangible benefits and rewards. Key scholars advocating for this approach include Roger Finke (American, 1954–) and Rodney Stark (American, 1934–).

Religion: This is the formal, systematic expression of supernatural beliefs, practices, rites, behaviors, and associated moral codes.

The Sacred: According to French Sociologist Émile Durkheim (1858–1917), the sacred refers to all collective religious ideas and artifacts that transcend nominal social life.

Sacro-Clericalism: Individuals from this people-group embrace organized religion in the form of common creeds and doctrinal positions, the definition and development of denominational movements, even the construction of church buildings and offices—all detailing what it means to be a Christian, at least legitimately and corporately.

Sacro-Communalism: Individuals from this people-group avoid official organized events and regular meetings as being too political and contrived; they prefer an informal way of religious life that is far removed from the hyperactive, rigid halls of institutional church, preferring the coffee shop to the sanctuary.

Sacro-Egoism: Individuals from this people-group embrace the idea that the self (or the ego) has the highest sacred authority in a person's life, giving direction and meaning to religious and spiritual activities (or non-participation); for these people, God and religion are seen more as "helpers" to individual spiritual fulfillment in life.

Sacro-Theism: Individuals from this people-group include anyone who gives primary authority to mystical encounters and directly perceived revelation from God; they downplay the authority of human authority (individual or corporate) and suggest that all true beliefs have their origin and affirmation in and from God.

Scholasticism: Embraced and advanced in European universities through the writings and teachings of historical figures such as Anselm of Canterbury (English, 1033–1109 CE), Peter Lombard (Italian/French, 1095/1100–1160 CE), and Thomas Aquinas (Italian, 1225–1274 CE), this movement attempted to reconcile and align Medieval Christian scholarship and thought with the philosophy and teachings of ancient Greco-Roman scholars, et al.

Secularization: This is a religious theory proposed in modernity suggesting that, for many people, Christianity (especially in the Western world) is losing its social power and influence to areligious groups and agents, with people seeking out and utilizing non-religious offerings as a substitute for traditional religious services. Key scholars advocating for this approach include Bryan Wilson (British, 1926–2004) and Steve Bruce (Scottish, 1951–).

Spiritual Revolution Theory: This postmodern religious theory suggests that people are abandoning mainstream religions and beliefs for alternative spiritual practices such as found in the New Age Movement, Astrology, homeopathic practices, and the Holistic Milieu. Key scholars advocating for this approach include Wade Clark Roof (American, 1939–), Grace Davie (British, 1946–), and Linda Woodhead (British, 1964–).

Spirituality: This concerns one's beliefs or praxis surrounding a personal sense of non-material, transcendent reality or forces that can be perceived and encountered in human existence. Due to its focus of the non-worldly, non-empirical, nuanced aspects associated with spirituality, scientific study is extremely difficult and controversial.

Traditionalism: This is the belief that historical human conventions, including religious ones, come only from divine revelation and should be honored, obeyed, and protected from progressive, human deconstruction and/or destruction.

Discussion Questions

1. What cultural developments in the 19th and 20th centuries challenged traditional Christianity's doctrinal and social positions in Western society? What was the most significant factor and why?

2. How has radical individualism in American society since the 1960s affected religious life? What do you think will ultimately happen to religious life in America in the future?

3. Which of the Sacro-States do you identify with the most? Why? What about for your parents and grandparents?

4. Discuss the differences between Rational Choice Theory, Secularization Theory, and the Spiritual Revolution Theory. Which one do you think is the most relevant to American religious culture (and why)?

5. Discuss your understanding of the person of God. How does your perspective compare to that of Hollywood's depiction and understanding of God in the movies and television?

Suggested Sources

Alexander, M. (2010). *The new Jim Crow: Mass incarceration in the Age of Colorblindness.* New York, NY: The New Press.

Allport, G. (1979). *The nature of prejudice: 25th anniversary edition.* USA: Perseus books.

Beckner, H. (1963). *Outsiders: Studies in the sociology of deviance.* New York, NY: The Free Press of Glencoe.

Berger, P. (1963). *Invitation to sociology: A humanistic perspective.* New York, NY: Doubleday.

Blumer, H. (1986). *Symbolic interactionism: Perspective and method.* USA: University of California Press.

Bourdieu, P. (1984). *Distinction: A social critique of the judgment of taste.* Cambridge, MA: Harvard University Press.

Carmichael, S. (1971). *Stokely speaks: Black power back to pan-Africanism.* New York, NY: Random House.

Comte, A. (1976). *The foundation of sociology.* London, UK: Nelson.

Connell, R. (1983). *Which way is up?: Essays on sex, class, and culture.* Sydney, New South Wales: Allen & Unwin.

Cooley, C. (2015). *Mind, self, & society.* Chicago, IL: University of Chicago Press.

Cumming, E., & Henry, W. (1961). *Growing old: The process of disengagement.* New York, NY: Basic.

Doob, C. (2013). *Social inequality and social stratification in U.S. Society.* Upper Saddle River, NJ: Pearson.

DuBois, W.E.B. (1994). *The souls of Black folk.* U.S.A.: Dover.

Durkheim, E. (2008). *The elementary forms of religious life.* Oxford, UK: Oxford University Press.

Durkheim, E. (1979). *On suicide: A study in sociology.* New York, NY: The Free Press.

Durkheim, E. (1982). *The rules of sociological method and selected texts on sociology and its method.* New York, NY: The Free Press.

Frank, A. (1967). Capitalism and underdevelopment in Latin America: Historical studies of Chile and Brazil. *Monthly Review Press, 2*(3), 361.

Garfinkel, H. (1967). *Studies in ethnomethodology*. USA: Prentice Hall.

Giddens, A. (1986). *The constitution of society: Outline of the theory of structuration*. USA: University of California Press.

Goffman, E. (1959). *The presentation of self in everyday life*. New York, NY: Anchor.

Goffman, E. (2009). *Stigma*. New York, NY: Touchstone.

Havighurst, R. (1972). *Developmental tasks and education*. Boston, MA: Addison-Wesley Longman.

Hoffer, E. (1951). *The true believer: Thoughts on the nature of mass movements*. New York, NY: Harper Perennial Modern Classics.

Hughes, E. (1984). *The sociological eye: Selected papers (social science classics series)*. New York, NY: Routledge.

Hull, P. & Hull, R. (1969). *The Peter principle*. New York, NY: William Morrow and Company.

Jung, C. (1976). *The portable Jung*. New York, NY: Penguin.

Knox, J. (2016). *Sacro-Egoism: The rise of religious Individualism in the West*. Eugene, OR: Wipf & Stock.

Linton, R. (1959). *The tree of culture*. New York, NY: Vintage.

Marx, K., & Engels, F. (2012) *The Communist manifesto: A modern edition* (2nd Edition). New York, NY: W.W. Norton.

Martineau, H. (2016). *How to observe: Morals and manners*. USA: Jefferson.

Mead, G. (1936). *Movements of thought in the nineteenth century*. Chicago, IL: University of Chicago Press.

Merton, R. (1951). *Social theory and social structure*. New York, NY: The Free Press.

Mills, C. W. (1967). *The power elite*. Oxford, UK: Oxford University Press.

Mills, C. W. (1967). *The sociological imagination*. Oxford, UK: Oxford University Press.

Myrdal, G. (1944). *An American dilemma: The Negro problem and modern democracy*. New York, NY: Harper & Brothers.

Ogburn, W. (1964). *William F. Ogburn on culture and social change, selected papers*. Chicago, IL: University of Chicago Press.

Omi, M. & Winant, H. (1986). *Racial formation in the United States* (1st Edition). New York, NY: Routledge.

Parsons, T. (1967). *The structure of social action*. New York, NY: Free Press.

Piaget, J. & Inhelder, B. (2000). *The psychology of the child*. New York, NY: Basic Books.

Ritzer, G. (1993). *The McDonaldization of society (8th edition)*. USA: Sage.

Rogers, E. (1994). *A history of communication study: A bibliographical approach*. New York, NY: Free Press.

Sapir, E. (2004). *Language: An introduction to the study of speech (Dover language guides)*. USA: Dover.

Simme, G. (1972). *On individuality and social forms*. Chicago, IL: University of Chicago Press.

Sutherland, E. (1985). *White collar crime: The uncut version*. New Haven, CT: Yale University Press.

Taylor, F. (1903). *Shop management*. New York, NY: American Society of Mechanical Engineers.

Turner, R. & Killian, L. (1987). *Collective behavior*. Upper Saddle River, NJ: Pearson.

von Bohm-Bawerk, E. (2015). *Capital and interest: A critical history of economical theory*. London, UK: Andesite Press.

Wallerstein, I. (1974). *The modern world system: Capitalist agriculture and the origins of the European world economy in the sixteenth century*. New York, NY: Academic Press.

Washington, B. T. (1963). *Up from slavery: An autobiography*. Garden City, NY: Doubleday.

Weber, M. (1978). *Economy and society: An outline of interpretive sociology*. Vol. 1 & 2. USA: University of California Press.

Weber, M. (2010). *The Protestant ethic and the spirit of Capitalism*. Oxford, UK: Oxford University Press.

Whorf, B. (1956). *Language, thought, and reality: Selected writings*. USA: University of California Libraries.

Wirth, L. (1956). *The ghetto*. Chicago, IL: University of Chicago Press.